BURNT OFFERINGS

BURNT OFFERINGS

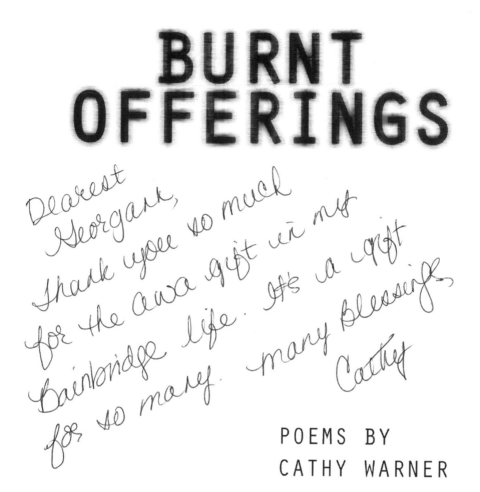

Dearest Georgann,
Thank you so much
for the awa gift in my
Bainbridge life. It's a gift
for so many. Many Blessings,
Cathy

POEMS BY
CATHY WARNER

eLectio Publishing
Little Elm, TX
www.eLectioPublishing.com

*For my husband Kevin, and daughters Jennifer, and Chrissy,
and for my soul sisters Becky and Tarah (whose painting graces this cover):*

Your love, encouragement, and creative genius inspire me.

TABLE OF CONTENTS

I Want a Voice Like Billy Collins

One of his books sits on my bedside table
Each night I allow myself one poem
restraining from gluttony
the same way I trained myself
away from a whole bag of M&M's
in favor of one tiny square
of the darkest chocolate I can find

It is after all poetry and I want
to do it right savor it like a guilty pleasure
tasting on my tongue the unadulterated
cowness of his Irish cows the steaming
locomotive perfection of his cigarettes
the Beethoven symphony of his neighbor's dog

There's some chemical in chocolate
released in the body the same way his poems
dissolve in my mind something I'm sure
that could be explained in the kind of book
I'd never read

I finger the spine of *Picnic Lightning*
wonder if I slid it under my pillow
while I slept if osmosis would have
its way with me if upon waking
my head would be filled with
fresh baked scones, blackberry preserves
and clotted cream that would pour
onto the page a diapered baby poem
with a startling cry

Possessed

You are crazy with the itch of people
parading through your head.
They shout through breakfast and aerobics and laundry
until you write them out of your ears and eye sockets
talk them down ladders onto paper.

They tap you on the shoulder
during intimate marital moments
and laugh when you shoo them away.
They don't sleep, rest or disappear,
obnoxious and complaining,
every last one of them,
even the sweet old lady who lives in the right brain.

You wash dishes and they talk to you.
Tell me again, how did you describe my dress?
They make you repeat phrases in your head
over and over until you explode words.
Then they say, you've got it wrong,
the dress was periwinkle and not lavender, after all
and the difference is incredibly huge.
The difference is what stands between you
and the garbage disposal and the National Book Award.

But your writing time is over.
You have responsibilities, and a family: *real people*
you remind the pathetic creatures that live in your head.
They don't care.
Mrs. Right Brain wants gin and a dented primered Impala
You can't possibly, you tell her, *that's so out of character.*

It's time to help your daughter with her homework:
If Sam has twenty-seven shirts, and twelve of those shirts are white
and another six are green, calculate
the percentage of Sam's shirts that are blue.

You think Sam should calculate his own damn shirts.
Speaking of shirts, says Mrs. Right Brain
I'd like one of those gauzy ones with bells on the sleeves.

Get a life, you tell her then yourself.
You had a life but it's been appropriated permanently.
It terrifies you to think in this manner:
You are not one for chronic conditions,
terminal diseases, or permanent relationships.

Now this nagging backache, puffy-eyed
sleep-robbing disease has taken residence
underneath your pores inside your cells.
This thing, demons, or creativity, or writing
will live curled at the base of your skull,
stretching tendons into your brain pan,
the absolute rest of your possessed life.

You turn to Mrs. Right Brain and ask,
How about a nice Toyota?

Becoming Blackfish

According to Native legends, the blackfish (orcas)
were once humans who took to the water

I want nothing between me
and the moon-driven tide
the morphing sky
and the chameleon water
but the thin skin
I would peel down
and cast off
as I slip into the blue
and fin away
free

Don't Walk

I cling to my misery as if
it were my only possession.
My tattered cardboard sign
the only constant I can grasp.
Look at my suffering
inked in big black letters.
I want to scream and stomp
shout it from the corner
where I stand watching
commuters flood onramps.

I am stuck at the intersection
hemmed in by speeding traffic
waiting for someone to yield
someone to give me the right of way.
No one slows. No one stops.
My fingers ache from holding
the sign of distress.
My toes cramp, my feet ache.
My soles grow weary.

I am waiting, not patiently
but full of anger and anguish.
Wanting the green light
the go ahead. Wanting someone
speeding in his four-door sedan
to give me a break. Stop or yield
wave me permission to cross
even though I don't know
my destination
or the direction I'm headed.

I stare at the opposite corners eyeing
each red hand on its metal pole,
anxious for one, any one to change
into a pedestrian glowing white
and confident lit up
in its electronic box.

Maybe a countdown too
flashing numbers indicating
how much time
has been allotted for me
to cross safely.

Thirty or forty seconds
when my passage is protected
when I'm not forced
to contend with two tons of metal
and a distracted driver
bearing down on me.
But there's no guarantee
someone won't run
a red light
and rage at me
for failing to jump
out of the way fast enough
cursing me for my very existence.

So I stand on the corner
anxious as a rabbit
preparing to dash between
a coyote and a bobcat
believing it is life or death
as dire as all that.
Despite the adrenaline
I am frozen. Trapped
on my concrete island.
The signal cycles
and cycles and never
issues my invitation to cross.

Alone and stranded
I have failed
to push the walk button.

Zeke and the Dry Bones

Inspired by Ezekiel 37

Zeke borrows a trick from God
Puts on a record
Makes dry bones dance
In my living room

Zeke divines blood
And bone between us
When what exists
Are brittle fragments
Best left unexhumed

He tries to strip us
From love's grave clothes
I want to believe he can

My flesh and bone
Long to dance
In the living room
Sinewy breath
Pulsing blood
Revived by Zeke's bones

The record skips
The beat is off
Zeke's sharp elbows
And bony protrusions
Jab

We fall
Flesh away
Revealing the valley
Between us
Prophetless and bone dry

Revelations

For Rev. Sandra Hammett

There are a thousand ways to shatter
but those well trained in theater
plaster on smiles
bind wounds to our chests
wear sunglasses indoors
and take the stage

Until God enters
our dressing rooms mid-run,
opens the blinds
and pushes us fully clothed
into the shower.

When I was drowning
Jesus came to me
dressed as the Gorton's fisherman
in yellow squall slicker and hat.

He appeared to you in Vegas vision:
Rhinestone-studded suit, strutting on a white stallion,
the lost souls riding posse behind him.

Either way, there are a thousand ways
Jesus kneels, retrieving our scattered pieces.
The house lights go on,
we give up the act.

I Used to Believe

I used to believe
I could earn brownie points
from the universe
sorting my recycling:
cans from glass from plastics from paper.
I used to believe
in being an earth-mother
catching my waiting-for-it-to-get-hot
shower water in a bucket
and lugging it to the garden
to water my three rose bushes.
I used to believe
in guilt as the motivating source
reusing my disposable plastic cups
until they cracked apart.
I used to believe
forgiveness was soft,
useless as a saturated paper towel.
I used to believe
a God who created woman
from a rib was laughable.

I believe now
that brownies are only for eating
even though I still recycle.
I believe now
in an Earth-father and a God-mother
and the other way around
and every which way in between.
I believe now
in love that overflows
any cup
washing away needless guilt.
I believe now
in something more—
it happened the day my shower water
turned to love
the day Jesus
handed me a towel.

I believe now
that forgiveness
is the boldest act
in our universe.
I believe now
that the slat
between our ribs
is the perfect place
to carry our faith.

We All Sit Beside a Pool of Tears

For Rev. Trevor Hudson
and the Companions in Ministry community

We all sit beside a pool of tears
Mine was home to algae and mosquitoes
not much more than a puddle, really
I sat there everyday unable
to see the sun, the moon, or myself
reflected in the murk, hoping
for a tadpole to take up residence
or dew to float on a leaf

The dark immensity of tears beside you
was too deep to fathom
too wide to sail across
the rain of accumulated pain
tsunamis of sorrow, centuries of grief

Unlike me, you didn't sit at water's edge
helpless, hoping

You braved the stagnant sea
waded until you submerged
our despair alive against your skin
Your nostrils flared, your mouth opened
you did what those of us desperate
to survive avoid

You gulped in our grief
drowned in the lake of our shatteredness
then you emerged, coughing, sputtering
the weight of us dripped
from your robe and beard

You stroked toward shore
then stopped, knelt
The pool now clear glittering
lapped at your chest

You beckoned to us
we who stood on the sand
thinking we had witnessed your folly

Tentatively we inched closer
Shivering in the shimmering wet
You touched our shoulders
cupped the small of our backs
dunked us into Presence
We surfaced, soaked and stunned

You wiped our eyes
scooped up our tears
held your palms to our lips
We bent and drank

The Edge of Your Life

When you come to the edge of all that you know,
you must believe one of two things:
either there will be ground to stand on,
or you will be given wings to fly.
–O.R. Melling, *The Summer King*

When you come to the edge of all you know
you might drop into a chasm a thousand feet
down before you crash onto a ledge sturdy enough
to hold you. From there it is up to you whether
you wither or whether you kick and test and gouge
footholds until your nails are ripped, your fingers
cracked and bloody, whether you trust yourself
to inch up a precipice and not look down.

It's all that backward glancing that causes you to slip
lose your grip, bruise your tailbone, fracture a rib, shatter
your confidence. It's all those scabs torn open over again
those festering wounds that convince you the world
is not safe, that scaling your personal Mount Everest
is not possible. But really, it is, despite past experience.
You don't always end frozen in ice, oxygen canisters
discarded at your feet.

There is a weightless present moment when each grain
of granite glints before you, when you become intimate
with its surface, one square inch at a time, when your momentum
can only be measured in millimeters. Truly (truly he said
to us) it doesn't matter if the movement is imperceptible
if the climb takes all of your life. Why shouldn't it?

Forget learning to fly, forget everything but faith. Just breathe
and grab and pull and breathe and launch yourself
off the edge of your life into the unknown—gritty
with possibility.

Shaped

I am reaching for a metaphor
to describe not only what happened
but what those happenings mean
how they marked and carved
and shaped without my knowing

This existential sculpting
it is a subterranean language
that comes to mind
but nothing so grand as core,
magma and mantle,
nothing as violent as volcano
as earthshaking as quake

Something much more subtle
like centuries of continental drift
the slow parade of plate tectonics
as we float past each other unaware

I gaze down on my life
as if from canyon rim and only now
does the past become visible:
striations of sedimentary rock
the subtle insistent layering
of experience

earth and water, erosion and silt
glacial creep and spring melt
the cliff face made smooth
the hidden life exposed
the narrow path revealed

Waiting for Someone To Unlock the Church Where I Will Preach My First Sermon

In the garden outside stucco walls
white pincushions bloom their leaves
like fingers in a glove beckoning
from centers spiked with yellow.

A fly hovers shiny and black
cellophane wings rumbling in place,
a holding still but not.
In the moment before
it steps with lash thin feet
everything in the body vibrates:
I am here I am alive.

I wait on an aggregate bench
sitting bones pressed against rock
while traffic on the expressway
rushes through my ears
and wind whips my hair into my mouth
chilling me through.
It is too cold for one who is neither flower nor fly.

I am perched stiff, like the wooden cross
anchored to the roofline above me.
When the sun extends its arms, I unfold mine
and lift my face toward the hawk
gliding against the cloud-pocked sky
and propel myself toward the divine.

I will not come to it hard like rock against bones
or rigid like cross against pinnacle.
I will come on outstretched wings
in the almost still of a thermal current.

As intricate and unknowable as a single petal
the mystery on which I hope to alight.

Death Is a Bargain

The local graveyard is full of little altars
plastic roses and daisies, Kewpie dolls
and Superman action figures (at my brother-in-law's grave).

It's like walking the aisles at Pic 'N Save stacked
with 59-cent ceramic vases standing askew, curlicues chipped.
All these lives broken and cracked mishandled decayed
but I thumb through the gaudy photo frames and poorly
illustrated prints anyway, hoping despite the evidence
I might find something beautiful
and useful on the bargain shelves.

I stroll slowly among the headstones wondering
how to price a life. What is the value of a year?
Does a young death always cost more?
Is an elder always twenty-five percent off?
And after it's over do the dead even care?

I find a morbid satisfaction in impressing people
with how little I paid in life...
You like it? I bought it half-off of $4.99 at K-Mart.

Is that how it will be at my end—plucked
from the bargain bin by God's meaty thumb—
slightly defective but still serviceable?

I suppose I must brag that it took so little
on my part to buy me eternity.

The Art of Fermentation

I don't have what it takes
to make *kombucha*
I can't ferment tea in a clean mason jar
on my kitchen windowsill
without *The Mother.*
But where do I find her
this brown jellyfish matriarch
this *mushroom*
her bloom the essential
ingredient in tea's transformation?

At the natural foods store
colorful kombucha sparkles
in clear glass pints
bottled and labeled
by a man named GT Dave
who writes that he first
brewed the concoction
to nourish his mother
wasting from cancer.

Is she sitting now
at her sunny kitchen table
GT at her side
clinking mugs?
Does she lick foam from her upper lip
while they laugh
at the way her misfortune
became his fortune?
Does she smile as she swirls
the thin strands
of the mother
at the bottom of her cup?

Or is this all that is left
of the mother—his mother
these grainy threads
this storied label?

Serving My Father Communion

For my father

In the new Protestant liturgy
we offer the bread of life
and dip into the cup of promise.

We think less about Jesus on the cross
and more about the new covenant
he preached in that upper room
sharing the Passover meal with his best friends
even the one who would betray his trust.

It's one way we try to make this ancient
Lord's Supper, this Communion that we forget
to call *Holy* mean something
in our sanitized, ordered, and solitary lives.

We don't like the old words
too earthy, too gory
to talk about the body broken
and the blood poured out
for me and for you
and for many
for the forgiveness of sins.

We don't want to go there
to the confession
to the admission
to the introspection
that our lives might require forgiveness.

We simply want a spiritual boost
a pinch of bread
a quick dip into the cup.
We chew; we swallow.
We resume our seats.

On this particular Sunday
I hold the loaf in both my hands
and the people come to me.
One by one
they rip a piece from the whole
until it is my father standing
before me.

My father, a former altar boy
a long-lapsed Catholic who left
my mother when I was nine.
This is the first time we have
set foot in church together.

I had believed my faith did not
come from him. But here he is
standing before me bridging
years of distance. I look at
his face—past cancer's ravages
to find the father I remember
and I reach back for the old words:

*This is the body of Christ
given in love for you.*

My father pinches a portion
holds it between his fingers
inclines his face
and offers me his lips.

This is my body they relate.
And you are my blood.

We kiss and I know
the words of my mouth
are true.

This is the body
risen from one yeast
formed from one dough
torn from one loaf
given out of and into love
for you and for me
for my father and for many
for the forgiveness
of all that is needed.

Sestina for Scissors & Thread

In my former life I used to sew.
Buy a pattern, choose material,
select notions, zipper and thread,
cut pattern, baste and gather
ruffled sleeves and skirts. Seam
at ten stitches per inch. Wear clothes.

In this life I mend clothes,
patch knees and reunite buttons. I sew
tears in pants and rips at the seam.
Stashed under my bed is material.
Scraps my daughters now gather.
They fasten doll clothes with thread

or Scotch tape and imaginary thread
transforming remnants into clothes.
Patches of imagination I gather
to prevent fading in time so
I save tiny squares of life's material
in my sewing basket. I seem

to recall our quilt. A running seam
binds us with familial thread.
Well-worn material
thin beauty knits us close,
wraps us in this family, so
we pull it tight and gather

tomorrow. Each season we gather
the bounty of harvest. Then seem
to wait for the seeds we sow
to bear fruit. We thread
and cut through days. At their close
we reflect on the material.

Stories of our lives. Raw material
woven into fabric we gather
then pattern, cut and wear. Clothes
created for this journey. We seem
blissfully unaware of eternal thread
connecting one to another, so

we embroider material and work a seam.
Gather stitches with matching thread.
Not clothes, but beloved story quilt, we sew.

The Texture of Spring

For my daughters

This is the texture of spring:
redwood forest fresh with rain
greening of the wild world.
Forget-me-nots and miner's lettuce
propagating near storm drains
and road shoulders.

The sun returning from winter's absence
below the tree line, like Persephone
to her mother. Daffodils craning
toward the weak sun.

Me with a swollen belly
pushing forth new life
from muted and muffled loam.
Lion and lamb lying together
giving birth to the young
and their mothers alike.

Spiny frond and translucent skin,
spongy mushroom and infant pudge.
My daughters, heads downy
as newly-hatched blue jays,
tucked in the nest of my arms.
Nursing blisters and breasts
swollen like rivers with snowmelt.

This is the desire of spring:
to split open and suck every last drop.
To swallow the seeds and sing
beneath the midnight sky.
The tidal ebb that lulls and soothes you,
the rocker's glide on the bedroom floor,
and the open heart
that devastates and transforms you.

Things That Are Beautiful

In the tradition of "The Pillow Book" by Sei Shonagon of Japan, written in 1002

The bottomless blue of a glacial pool surrounded by craggy walls of ice.

Crackled frost on fallen leaves plastered to the hood of one's car.

Twelve pounds of purring tabby cat nestled on one's lap.

The glistening red nursing blister visible on a baby's upper lip in sleep.

Wax stalactites formed by candles dripping in a sanctuary on a Sunday morning.

A mile-long ribbon of Mexican free-tailed bats looping across Austin in the summer dusk.

The top-forty song one sings while showering and chopping onions that is secretly a love song to God.

The sound of one's name whispered in the dark low and soft as a caress.

The exhale—loud and forceful as a hundred tired men—of an orca surfacing off San Juan Island.

Gleaming raspberries in a clear glass bowl and a cherished friend to savor them with.

One who holds open a door, physical or metaphorical, for one who is burdened, physically or metaphorically.

The music of the Holy Spirit that trills up one's spine like fingers on piano keys.

Any flower painted by Georgia O'Keefe that entices one to become a bee, crawl inside, and suck out the nectar.

The perma-bruised rice-paper skin of the grandmother's hand one holds.

Remembering My Grandmother

Jesus talks to me in stories because I am
like his old friends around Galilee a little slow on the uptake.
"Sit down," he says and I join him on the lawn
under the cherry trees while pink petals flutter to the ground.
He knows that I already know the image of how he'd like to gather us
under wing like a mother hen, but that being raised in the suburbs
perhaps it's not the best metaphor for me.

So he tries it again with a different slant.
"Cathy," he says, "God is like this—
Your eighty-nine-year-old grandmother dying
in her hospital bed, brittle as a baby chick
who pecked her way back to consciousness
whenever a doctor, nurse, or chaplain entered the room
who opened her milky eyes and said with all the pride
she could muster, 'Have you met my granddaughter?
She came all this way just to see me.'
And then, satisfied that the world knew how precious and beloved
you are, she drifted back into the world between worlds."

Jesus stands, brushes the blossoms from his hair and walks away.
As he disappears from view, my first thought is
that he is inordinately fond of poultry, but then I remember
that my grandmother did have a bantam hen in her backyard
when I was a little girl.
Back then I visited her for a week every summer. She bought me
the Lucky Charms cereal my mother never would and took me
to wondrous places—Griffith Observatory and Chatsworth Park.

I thought I had gone to my grandmother's bedside
to minister to her in her last days, singing hymns while I kept vigil.
Instead, just like always, I was welcomed, blessed
and made holy by her love.

Transfiguration

I have seen transfiguration
a young woman lit up with new love
the radiant smile of a groom
the inner glow of a pregnant woman
beaming parents, a newborn child
the long-married luminous and dancing under the moon
the light that gentles us from this life into the next.

Each brush with love transforms us
if only temporarily and like the sun
it burns so bright we must look indirectly or go blind.
We can only come so close to the Great Source
before we catch fire from the inside out.
Like Moses our beards shimmer
Like Jesus our garments blaze white.
This is transformation—
shining from the mountaintop
in momentary perfection
dumbfounding those in our presence.

As the blush fades we descend from the peaks
to the plains of our existence
uttering our small prophecies.
We are no longer dazzling or set apart
but, oh, we have been changed.

There Is Yes

Time wears her mother's rosary and sits cross-legged
with the Virgin Mary. She leafs through seasons, faded photos
and yellowed pages, scatters her bounty like windfall apples
across the acres of this ordinary story.

This story, this history unfolded when eyes looked long
across a kitchen table and coffee cups danced on green Formica.
There was a cough, a question, a mute suspense of future
sandwiched between row crops, roosters, and barking dogs.

The answer must have been *yes*. How could it be otherwise?
For there are petal-soft apricots and thorny artichokes
sold at roadside stands. There are blisters formed
in fields, knees caked in mud, and the gathering of words.

There are Sundays of lipstick and Mass, starched collars and menudo.
Infants baptized and pan dulces eaten in aluminum-awning shade.
There is the monotonous wonder of days
and the infinite sameness of nights.

Callused fingers dose aspirin and knead bad backs
pay electric bills and pack lunches in brown paper.
In backseats, teenagers grope—music too loud.
And everywhere the sweet secret making of babies.

There is waking to the smell of warm pajamas folded
under a pillow and the gargling hum from the shower
unwashed dishes in the sink and creaky couch springs.
Of course the answer was *yes*.

Without *yes*, there is no ease at the end of a shift
and the dusty drive home leads somewhere outside
this story. But there is *yes* and this telling and beyond
it breathes the other half of a life. A prayer unspoken.

The Marriage Feast

For Laura and Bob Burnett

It starts with an introduction
a handshake and hello
a small kindness
that anyone would extend
to anyone else.

And then it becomes
specific, particular—
the sound of his voice
the shape of her laugh
the heart leaping
into the stomach
when the other
calls your name

And later it sticks a toe
in the water
tentative and testing
because who hasn't been there before?
Who hasn't placed their
fragile trust in the hands
of another
only to find it slip
and shatter
only to be left heartbroken
clutching a broom and dustpan
sweeping up pieces of themselves?

And then it dawns
the way morning colors
imperceptible but unmistakable
and you are more than okay
more than fine by yourself
more than you can contain
so you open your fist
and stretch out your fingers
intertwining them with the one
you call Beloved.

Every day together
you rise like bread
a yeast fermenting
something new between you.
And yes you are flattened
and yes you are punched down
and yes you are rolled and stretched
and shaped into someone stronger
more resilient and more expansive
than you've ever been before.

And so it comes to this
right here right now
an eternal declaration to this truth.
Love is exploding all around us
showering down on you and me
shimmering like sunset on ocean
branding its image in our eyes.

Love is talking despair
down from the ledge
and onto the sidewalk
where the crowd has gathered.

Love is walking through the streets
handing out silvery thin blankets
hot rolls and steaming coffee in disposable cups.
One by one we reach for
what Love has to offer
and then we pass the platter.

Ash Wednesday

Soon I will be marked
smudge of ashes
across my forehead
gritty remains of fire
smeared on my skin
a small grating
anticipated

I don't absorb them
the soot and the meaning
of the moment
as deeply as I desire
What more do I
long for as Lent
lengthens before me

Seraphim and the bite
of coal against my lips
the taste of fire
lighting my tongue
searing me into
proclamation

The Anointing

Think about the time you were nine
and walked downtown to the Rexall
to buy your mother a birthday gift.
A five-dollar bill
a month of mowing the lawn
folded flat in the front pocket
of your shorts.

Remember how you lingered over the colognes
Perused the aisle with its rows of boxed fragrances
lined behind a glass bottle, slender or squat, square or cylindrical
with a gold ball a top, or a silver spiked lid, or a plastic cubed cap,
all labeled seductively, *Tester*.

So you of course tested
although you knew Windsong was her favorite.
A dab of that inside your wrist
a splash of Jean Nate inside your elbow
a spritz of Love's Baby Soft mid-ulna
a squirt of wild strawberry three freckles up
a spray of Jovan Musk between tendons.
You proceeded from one arm sticky with scent
to the other
sniffing citrus and oak, steel and pine
as if you were a connoisseur of the pastel boxes
reading *parfum* and *toilet water*
which sent laughter snorting out your nose.

Remember how you had it gift wrapped
for free in silky pink paper with a silver foil bow.
The angles smoothly taped where yours
would've been lumpy and crooked.
You walked home, white bag in hand with its Rx emblazoned,
humming the commercial.
I can't seem to forget you. Your Windsong stays on my mind.

Recall how later you slid into the backseat of the Volkswagen
on the way to The China Moon, pink package on your lap.
And how, at the stop sign only four houses from home
when your father waited to make the turn onto Pacific Coast Highway
he wrinkled up his hawk nose
and glared in the rearview mirror.
What in the world is that smell?
You surreptitiously checked the bottoms
of your white strappy sandals
hoping you hadn't stepped in dog doo, again.
But then, you smelled it too,
there confined in the backseat with yourself
the unholy blend of Testers permeating out your pores.

Your mother laughed, her voice tinkling like ice in a glass
I guess you tried a few samples.
Your father cranked open his window
turned the corner and accelerated.
You leaned into the wind
hoping to escape the scent of yourself
vowing never to repeat the
odoriferous error of the fragrance aisle.

Now, think of Jesus
and that zealously emotional woman.
In the middle of a dinner party
while men lounge discussing the important issues of the day
she cracks open a flask
and pours an entire bottle of potent perfume
all over Jesus.
Sure it anoints him—
it cascades through his hair, runs over his brows into his eyes,
stinging and making the world look fuzzy.
It streaks his face like tears, drips through his forest of beard
slips down his neck
slides under and over his robes
tickling and trickling over his stomach and back.
I hate to be impolite, but he is sitting in nard!

It puddles around him.
A stream of perfume
a river of perfume
an ocean of perfume
it permeates his nostrils and consciousness.
The aroma fills her being.
The guests' palettes are ruined now.
Their noses overrun with nard, everything tasting like spice
and death and entirely wrong.

Think about after she stroked the perfume
into his hair and went home
after the commotion died down and the talk
of waste and poor had been settled.
Think about Jesus retiring that night—
a pungent guest in someone's home.
He was coated with his future, thick and greasy with portent.
How he must have tried to breathe above himself,
as if swimming to the surface
from a long submersion
wanting to gasp fresh untainted air
only to be thoroughly infused with his fate
his skin suffocating with knowledge.

Breathe in the bitter smell of death
from which there is no escape.
And then, once you've done all that
trace your fingers across the inside of your wrists
and see that the lash of ropes has vanished.
Press your nose to your skin and inhale
hard. Two or three times
until you believe
all things have been made new.

Pentecost

We can't outrun Pentecost
Hot breath of God on our faces
Spirit scorching our hair
One day it will singe off our eyebrows
and throw us into the street
on a tongue of flame

Pentecost comes to set us on fire
to brand what we know on our skin
to clean us to bone and sinew
The dove circles overhead
alights on our crowns
dares us to expose the spirit of things

How do we tell the world
we have been burnt down
blown away and recreated
How do we open our mouths
and let tumble out what we know
marrow deep

Someone has survived the burn
and danced in the ashes
This someone will stand with us
and keep sacred the space
at our center

It is the very emptiness that fills us
this void alive with fiery whirlwind
sweeps us into tornado dance

Shake up our lives
throw us off balance
refuse to set us down
until we arrive at Pentecost

Rowing Upstream

In Angola, the man who is eighty-six rows upstream
three hours to get home from church
his thin brown fingers laced over the almond colored oars.
He must sing hymns on the way,
stroking to the meter of an African *Amazing Grace;*
he's certainly found the sweet sound that will save him.

In his country, torn to shreds from twenty years of civil war,
orphans sleep in cardboard boxes, wandering the streets
of Luanda with its pink-domed capitol, and peddlers
sell toothbrushes from bins on their heads.

Surely the man hums as he paddles along the riverbanks
past grassy graves dotted with crosses. Even though the war
is over the killing continues––TB, Malaria, AIDS.
He is bold enough to sing *Jesus Loves Me* and wonder
at the strange way Jesus shows his love.
The man is old even by Western standards, and everyone
around him is dead, old and young alike.

He has no car, no bicycle, no televangelist to bring him
the Good News each week. He has no one but Jesus
and not some pocket-sized prosperity-gospel First World Jesus.

The old man's Jesus walks with orphans in the loud streets
of Luanda, cradling AIDs babies while they sleep.
The old man's Jesus breaks guns and buries their parts.
The old man's Jesus shows up in church, he likes the singing.
After the Sunday services, after the singing and the praying
and the reading of the Gospel, he walks through the flimsy walls
of the dilapidated building, climbs in the boat.

The old man's Jesus reaches for an oar and begins paddling.
The two of them pull in rhythm on the long trip home.

A Ranting Psalm

O God they say we are all your children
Created in your image, born into your eternal love
And I say to you—
What about those who abuse your children
Who force their sour breath upon innocent skin?

Too many of your children have suffered
At the hands of those who say they love them
Would it not be better if you destroyed with your own hand
Those who would destroy a childhood?

They say vengeance is yours
And I want to know if you're ever going to use it
If you're ever going to reach down
And press your hand against
The throats of the transgressors
Until the sounds of *don't tell anyone*
Are drowned in the gurgle of their spit
Silenced in their dying breaths.

I want what is right God
I want what is just
I want you to restore what has been stolen
From your daughters and your sons.

You will of course in time eventually
But why must the suffering last so long?

Sestina for the Sequoia Sempervirons

Hiking, we stand silently by
following flickers in the wood.
Our eyes find the deer
come to notch Vs in thick green
berry stalks growing wild there
among the branching trees.

We pass under oak trees
ground littered with acorns scattered by
wind and remember the Ohlone lived there
once but never slept beneath the redwood
that drips rain from needles green
and camouflages the deer.

You and I become winged, dear,
and nest atop towering redwood trees
two Marbled murrelets in a green
canopy. Endangered species hoping to buy
sanctuary from those who would
clear-cut our inheritance in their

lust to control the forest. There
is no hiding place for the deer
running naked in the wood.
They neither protest by climbing trees
nor lobby corporations that buy
old-growth groves with piles of green

pretending their policies are green.
The dealmakers applaud their
environmental colors by
ceremonial preservation of dear
land and our virgin trees.
Then come logging roads. We would

leave the city and save the wood
if we knew how to live off-grid and green.
As children we climbed backyard trees
with branches small as our dreams. But there
is an ancient connection we seek. Deer
jump across our path as we stream by

thinned wood masking scarred land over there.
The green forests reduced to myth and memory dear
we bid the trees, like dying acquaintances, a good bye.

Jackhammer

The jackhammer in the street
pierces, tears, breaks
what was solid
what seemed permanent
to repair the thing that lies
broken underneath
or to rip it away
all together
start over on raw ground
pour a new slab
a foundation built
on something better
something meant to last
this time around

Violent this construction
this creating
and recreating
whoever said
the hand of life
would be gentle

Leave Nothing Undared

Oblate Renewal Center, San Antonio, Texas

Leave nothing undared.

These are the words in bas-relief spurring
on the Oblates of Mary Immaculate. Life-sized
statues of sturdy men cast in bronze sit astride horses
crucifixes strung around their necks as they prepare
to ride into the vast expanse of Southern Texas

Preaching nothing but Christ crucified.

Specialists in the most difficult missions.

The memorial wall proclaims the deeds
of these Fathers who galloped the Word west.
I sit on the flagstone before them, pen in hand.
I am a specialist only in myself, thinking, as I
often and inevitably do, that it is all about me.
Then some men wearing clerical collars to proclaim
their vocation and wide brimmed hats to prevent
sunstroke galloped out of 1849 alongside the words

Strive to be saints.

On horses sweating and briny, they brought manna
to the poor and the Son crucified to the hungry.
And, slowly, no faster than the beast and spirit
could carry them, they rode the Word throughout
this continent and onto others.

Leave nothing undared.

The words flare at me like a mare's hot nostrils.
I have been pawing at my life stomping like a wild
colt confined, unable to get my own way, and unable
to live with myself not getting what I want. I buck
against the circumstances saddled on my back.
I refuse the spurs against my ribs urging me forward.
I kick up dirt, toss my head, neigh blame, refusing
to leave my dingy stall.

This weight on my back, this load I stagger under
is the yoke that should be light, the burden
that should be lifted because of the One who chose to

Leave nothing undared.

The One Pleasing and Beloved set aside his own will
to allow a greater will to reign. I cling to my will as though
it were saddle and bridle, rider and horse, sun and North Star.
I confine my life to a map, bristling against reality. A map
is not terrain. The contour of a life cannot remain a blot of ink.

Leave nothing undared

The Oblates demand. If they stepped out of bronze
into flesh, would I have the courage to follow them?
Would I allow a rider on my back to guide my journey?
Could I plod along sometimes trotting, sometimes
galloping, sometimes roped to a tree, not knowing where
I might end up?

I sit before the memorial wall and pray for equine sense.

Empty Me

Hey Jesus, what kind of troublemaker disturbs
worship like that, scattering coins, turning
over tables, whipping animals?

Go ahead, cause a scene, it'll only add fuel
to the fire. Play with matches––you get burned.
Weren't we all warned about bad boys like you?

So, why is it that I hope you'll cause trouble
in my neighborhood?

Break into my house! Ransack my life!

Throw away the relationships gone bad.
Dispose of the sour grapes,
stale decisions, moldy worries.
Toss the torn priorities, the rotten what-ifs.
Pry the shoulds and to-dos grimy
and stained from my fingers.

Turn me inside out, hold me upside down
and shake until all the unholy debris falls
from my pockets then burn it.

You who've put on new life, you
who wear Resurrection
like a clean white robe, scrub me to the bone
then let me rest.

Invite me to sit alongside you
for just a moment––the two of us
shiny and pink, expectant
and radiant in our empty tomb.

Was That You, Jesus?

Maybe you were standing at the door for a long time
for a very long time but I didn't see you
didn't hear you over the clattering footsteps
of all the people walking in and out of my life

Maybe you rang the buzzer but my wires were disconnected
Maybe I opened the door but someone else
brushed in past you so I dated him

Maybe you knocked but I never heard
because I wasn't home I hadn't yet learned
to live in that house my house
with the gaping hole where the soul was supposed to be

Maybe you knocked but I was too tired
or too busy to answer and you had to stop
for just a moment because your knuckles were bruised and bleeding

Maybe when I thought I heard you
it was only the echo of your last knock
so that by the time I made it to the door I thought
no one was there

Maybe I heard you knock and considered letting you in
but I'd hidden the key to the door of my heart
or maybe the lock had been broken too many times

Maybe you didn't really barge in
Maybe I'm the one who unscrewed the hinges
so that the door only looked closed

Maybe that's why it seemed like you showed up
all of a sudden and finally one small sharp rap
toppling the door and you didn't mind
walking in barefoot over the splinters

Safety First

Every bush is burning
wildfire on the loose
God emblazoned emboldened
everywhere the trees explode
the branches rain down flames
and you'd think that I would notice
covered in ash
choking on dust
eyes stinging with smoke
that God has kindled
and consumed the world.

But it is all too much for me.
I want a campfire
of little twigs
confined to a cement ring
maybe Smokey the Bear
some marshmallows on sticks
and a round of *Kumbayah*
led by a uniformed ranger
from exactly 8 to precisely 9 p.m.
on a Saturday night.

And if by chance a spark
should crackle and leap
from that fire pit onto the ground
at my feet
you know that I will automatically
stub it out with my shoe.

It's what I was taught early on.
Stay away from matches.
Don't play with fire.
You might burn down the house.

It is after all a perilous world
and I don't want to get singed.

Kindling

Did you ever try to make fire
when you were young
Rub two twigs together
sliding one across the other
rapid fire
hoping for ignition
that never came

Did anyone ever teach you
when you were twelve
and in Scouts or on a field trip
how fire was really made

Two sticks
one prone and pierced
the other sharp and spinning
this direction then that
burrowing its needle tip
into the fleshy wood of the other
scraps of dried grass and dead
moss thrown into the mix

Did you see it
the blue snap
eyelash thin sparking
through a strand of moss
like electric litmus paper
the neon flame a tentative quiver
then leaping bold toward its neighbors
setting them on fire

When did Jesus ignite
between your twiggy fingers
When did God-fire burn your throat
choking out words
settling in the hollow pit of you
like radioactive dye
leaving you aglow
even when the world is dark

Do you remember the ancient one
and how bravely she carried the burning branch
to her people and set it at their feet
and how in her language she told them
Behold, I bring you life

Do you remember the spirit fire
and how it charred away your old self
how it burst open the seeds
of the long dormant life at your core
the blue inferno searing into your brain
a vision of the possible

Do you understand—
You're the burnt offering

Deliver the God-sparked, Jesus-flamed
Spirit-fired whole and human
divinely flawed and made perfect
burning bush of you
straight into the arms
of this parched and arid world
this tinder dry world waiting to be engulfed
by the wildfire that is God

Then, in your ash and ember voice
speak to those who would be kindling
preach to those who would be fuel
and tell them this—

Behold, I bring you life

Let Go

Let go, let go, let go
is the message of the labyrinth
Not let go and let God
Not let go and trust me
simply let go

Hot purple geranium petals
litter the path beneath my feet
The bush too has let go
as all things must

My Dog at Rest

He gives himself to it completely
stretched out on his side
head resting on the carpet
now and again an ear may twitch
or his head will cock for an instant
to make sure he heard it right
and then when he has let down all his guard
surrendered completely to this place
and this time and his place in it

then he will roll on his back
hind legs splayed exposing his pink
furless belly vulnerable and open
ready to submit and ready to receive
my next command

I pet him softly again and again
and think this is how to pray

Gathered Up, Gathered In

Jesus walks through the neighborhood Sunday morning
calling us from our homes and our cares.
We follow behind dragging our worries
like shopping bags and red wagons,
jangling our woes like pocket change.
He's the Pied Piper and we can't help
but fall hypnotized by his flute.

Strange that we hear him over the buzz
of power mowers, the hiss of cappuccino makers,
the roar of TV sports, the pounding bass from car stereos.
Odd that he appeals to the hi-tech VP with shrinking stocks
and irritable bowel, and to the single parent
on food stamps renting a room in another family's house.
Strange, that we would gather at the corner church,
like he was Quik-Stop and we need a quart of milk,
a pack of cigarettes, a lottery ticket.

We are freshly showered, fresh from cancer, fresh
from divorce, fresh from college, fresh from Iraq.
This Jesus makes a place for us, we crowd next to him
on the pew, or in the folding chairs, take refuge
under the shelter of his wings, gathered up, gathered in.
Free in the moment, from the uncertainty
of what comes next. We pray, we sing, we listen.

We watch the sun stream through windows,
maybe stained glass, maybe not.
The shafts of light teem with dust motes
life abundant suspended in the air all around us.
Funny that before he gathered us, we shared
the illusion we were alone.

Mary's Statue in Her Garden

Mercy Center, Auburn, California

Mary's feet peek out from under her robe
long perfectly formed alabaster digits.
The toes I wish I had. Coveting, I take
another look and see imperfection.
Her baby toes are short, too short
for a woman who withstood so much.

There she is, barefoot and crowned
holding her baby like a gift
face out to the world.

It's plain to see, he has her feet.
Like mother, like son.
And I wonder if they know
the footsteps ahead of them.
Their blank marble stares won't reveal
if they see it coming.

Jesus is already offering himself
arms extended, palms flat, welcoming
the future. So unlike my baby-clenched fists.

But there is something else about his hands
something I can see only when I circle close.
The fingers of his left hand are missing.
Damaged—it seems right to assume—
by human mishandling.

I look at Jesus's serious mouth
and his infant lips utter the words
he was destined to speak all along—

This is my body. Broken for you.

Forging Ahead

Remembering Rev. Tarah Trueblood's ministry
at Boulder Creek United Methodist Church

We're all being hammered down
smashed flat, quivering red and molten
like silver in refiner's fire

We're all being punched and pushed
squashed, spun, dizzy and thrown
like clay on a potter's wheel

Maybe we should've kept our mouths shut
kept our noses in our books
kept our hands in the dishwater
kept our feet on the gas pedal
kept our lives settled, stable
and possibly, doubtfully, content

But we had to do it, look up
from our circumscribed lives
remove our rose colored glasses
pry our fingers from their death grip
around familiar's throat
and belt out those words

Melt me, Mold me

Who would've known asking for God
would be this messy, this ugly
leaving us purple and bruised
dumped into the unknown
Who would've known we're not in control

Whether we like it or not
whether we admit it or not
God always had hands all over us
fingers poking and prodding
hot breath in our faces
whispering, shouting
when we lost attention

You're mine

So there we were and here we are
forging ahead sharpening our trust
kneading our faith

How else are we going to become silver forks
spearing meaty portions of justice for the poor
How else are we going to become clay cooking pots
steaming with hope to feed the hungry

How else are we going to rise up and follow
telling our stories of transformation
from mound of slimy clay to communion cup
from chunk of ore to steeple bell

How else are we going to stare straight
into the world's face
shift our weight in the Creator's palms
and cry out

Fill me, Use me

and really mean it

Full Ablaze

She had chosen invisibility in this second life
burnt down from shining so brightly
in her first.
It seemed a wise and necessary choice
placing herself inside the bushel basket
safely extinguished.
But after some time she felt the ache
her cramped legs and pretzled arms
the stale air, the dull dark.
And so she pushed against the barrel
bruising her shoulders until finally
it toppled, leaving her out there
vulnerable, exposed.
It would take her a long time
years, perhaps, to remember how
to unfold herself, how to walk
through the streets and into a room
sparks flying from her hem
lighting those in her path until
all of them were awake
full ablaze.

Take Up Your Cross

We carry our crosses
hung from our necks
lashed round our shoulders
nailed to our feet

No wonder we smack into doorframes
knock over our neighbors
slam face down in the street

All that dead wood
weighing us down

If only we dared look up
we might see him this Christ
head wreathed in thorns
nail studded palms
inclined toward us

What if we each rose
took up our splintery cross
and bore it in our arms
like a broken gift

What if we each rose
took up our cross
and followed the one
who forms hope from dust

Fishing With Jesus

For Rev. Linda Prendergast and the clergywomen
of the California-Nevada United Methodist Church

Jesus stands on the beach in the early morning mist
wearing waders, jeans, and a plaid flannel jacket.
He waves me over with his pole, then casts out for surfperch.

Fishing, he says. *A little something I picked up*
from Simon and Andrew, James and John.
Give it a try, he tells me, but fails to provide rod and reel.

So I do it the only way I know how. I kneel
in the hard packed sand and dig up crabs with my fingers.
I rinse them in the milky surf fringe just before
it rushes back to sea, and place the glistening creatures
in the plastic bucket at Jesus's feet. Watching them scuttle
in six inches of water, he nods his approval.

Then his pole bends and jerks and Jesus wrestles in a whale.
He pulls the tangled fishing line from its baleen
blesses it and sends it home.

I can't thread a pole, bait a hook, or reel leviathans from the deep.
All I know is how to gather up the jellies washed
on the beach, how to claw crabs out of the sand,
how to rinse them clean, how to ease out their stories
and how to gentle them into the living water.

Jesus knows and says this—*What you can do, it's enough.*

But what happens later? I ask. *When the bucket tips over,*
when the jellies are caught up in the turbulent surf,
when the crabs tunnel frantically into hiding, what then?

It's up to them, Jesus says, *to remember and be thankful.*

He gathers his gear ready to move up the beach.
He nods then calls back over his shoulder. *Keep fishing.*

What He Said After Dinner

In a moment I am leaving you
In a moment I am gone
returning to the One from whom
I have come

It will be time for you to be lost without me
Time for you to wander the landscape
of your familiar only to find it
utterly desolate completely foreign

I can't tell you how to manage
how to create a life from ashes
only to say that you will do it

It is your nature to grasp
the limb of hope
hold fast against the river of events
that will sweep me away

When you arrive safe on the other shore
you will wail gnash your teeth curse
the one who made us

After you have blamed yourself
for what you did not do
you will catch sight of me
scratch your head and wonder
convinced that you are mistaken
that my return is impossible

Listen to your heart leap
with recognition
believe
In that moment the entire world
will change

Bless the Poet

Blessed be the poet and the poem and the one between them who has no words.
-Jeanette LeBlanc

Blessed be the poet, the one who pays attention, the one whose large vocabulary leads me to a dictionary where I look up *quotidian* and learn it means *ordinary*.

Blessed be the poet who taps at the ordinary sea salt glommed into the shaker and ekes a stanza, if not seasoning, from it. Something equally necessary sprinkling from her hand—something elemental that sets off a chemical reaction.

The salt embodied ignites the page, our brains, our entire lives a fuse, the whole of human history spilled there like grains of sodium chloride atop a potato, itself the source of another stanza about heritage and famine and the indomitable power of the human spirit.

Oh bless that poet when I have been sucked into status updates, my meme-forwarding cyber-friends overwhelming me with their captioned *quotidiana*, an inexhaustible film of hollow words that I devour as if they will nourish me even though I am never satiated, always hungry for something that only the poet can deliver, bless her.

She arrives like the pizza delivery boy, holding out a box heavy and damp with steam and dough, meat and sauce that has me salivating even before I have closed the door and opened that box, carefully lifting a stringy slice of moment to my mouth.

Bless and praise the poet as I chew on her words, digest her meaning, feel the fullness in my belly, hum satisfied as I wash and dry the silverware and plates.

So often I am the one shuffling through the charity line snaking its way along the gritty sidewalk to the almshouse, holding out my empty arms to receive the offering of a poem. In that dismal queue, staring at my shoes, afraid to look into the faces of the needy all around me, I fail to see that we, all of us, are walking in the dappled forest light, standing ankle deep in the rich hummus of life, each of us and everything we touch a simile, a metaphor.

Bless oh bless the poet and bless oh bless the poem and bless oh bless the destitute one who waits between them with no words of her own.

In the Beginning

In the beginning was Word
and Word was with us
formed from ashes, dust and breath
and not one thing came into being
without Word.

Word was fruitful and multiplied
birthing wrinkled and radiant Poem.
Poem ate of the apple and ventured
from the garden into the wilderness.

In the forest, Poem encountered Story.
Brave and sturdy Story journeyed with Poem
scattering on their trail knights, wolves
bears, and girls in red hoods
so that they would not be lost.

Spring arrived and they happened upon a meadow.
Poem flitted from blossom to bloom
and Story burst forth in riotous color.
From the nearby village they came.

Those hungry for Word plucked fragrant Poem
from low branches and gathered
perfectly tasty windfall Story from the dirt
carting them home in aprons and bushel baskets.

And they feasted on Word abundantly.
Once upon a times
recited by old men at the hearth after supper
sung by mothers at the foot of cradles.

So it was that Word dwelt among them
petals of Poem and husks of Story
stitched with leather thong
bound to become Book.

Book beckoned all saying,
Come unto me you with eyes to see,
ears to hear and tales to tell.
Come and feast.

And so they came to sit at the feet of Book
learning the ways of ever after.
As it was in the beginning is now
and ever shall be—Word without end.

Acknowledgments

These poems begin and end in community, written over a span of fifteen years from my first poetry class through the University of California at Santa Cruz extension and with the handful of students (whose names I no longer remember) who continued to meet at Jumpin' Java in Mountain View, to the greater United Methodist Church, where I was nurtured as a leader and poet by the Commission on the Status and Role of Women, the Upper Room Academy for Spiritual Formation and Companions in Ministry, to the California/Nevada Conference of the United Methodist Church, its clergywomen's association, Conference Lay minister program, Board of Laity, Layspeaker program, and my home congregation in Boulder Creek, California, where I was a member for twenty-five years and served as pastor for seven, to my new writing group in Puget Sound.

In these communities I was blessed and loved, supported and given every opportunity to deepen my faith and skills in expressing that faith through poetry, prayers, and preaching, and the writing workshops I lead for others to discover their own creativity through spiritual writing.

This book of poetry is an offering to all those living and those gone onward with whom I have had the privilege to share the spiritual and writing journey, no matter how brief our association. I thank the Upper Room editors at *Alive Now* and the *Rhythm and Fire* anthology, and the Porter Gulch Review who published a few of these poems previously.

I thank my husband Kevin and inspiring daughters Jennifer and Chrissy, as well as the families I was born to and absorbed into in this living laboratory of love, growth, and forgiveness we inhabit.

I heap gratitude on Tarah Trueblood, once my pastor and mentor, now soul sister over years and miles. Her inspiring painting *Black Over Fire* graces the cover of this book. Visit Trueblood Art Studio on Facebook for more of her work.

I am also thankful for the encouragement from my former pastors Paul Sweet, Ted Pecot, Lorraine McNeal, and Sandra Hammett. The Reverends Dwight Kintner and Clyde Vaughn left retirement to share ministry at Boulder Creek with me. Laura Devine Burnett, Christine Bakalis, and Charlene Beisner filled my soul and our sanctuary with music. Bishop Beverly Shamana and the Rev. Donna Fado Ivery first claimed my writing as a spiritual gift for the church.

I'm grateful to mentors and colleagues in ministry Linda Kelly-Baker, Tom and Martha Weathers and my lay ministry trainers and class, Laura Heffernan, Holly Hillman, Becky Goodwin, Perry Polk, Anne Schlesinger, Linda (Wiberg) Caldwell and the Board of Laity, and Robin Matthews-Johnson and my clergy covenant group.

Gifted writers have graced Boulder Creek United Methodist Church and my time there, especially Phyllis Mayfield, Catherine Marcotte, Einar Finstad, Linda Lininger, Kristin Centofante, and the late Judith Newton.

The Academy for Spiritual Formation leadership and journey-takers inspired my passion for writing, particularly Suzanne Seaton, Ginger and Wes Howl, Nancy Danson, Judy Bulman, Mary Blom, Jan Sechrist, Sue Magrath, and Emily Linderman.

The Companions in Ministry Writing Group shared and celebrated writing as essential to our vocation. Thank you Jerry Haas, Ann Scott, Johnny Sears, Roberta Egli, Pamela Hawkins, Eric Van Meter, Lisa Garvin, Chansoon Lim, Jane Herring, Bart Fletcher, and Luann Charlton.

I deeply appreciate the critique and encouragement of my prose by Kirby Wilkins, Natalie Serber, Doreen Devorah, Susan Drake, Jerry Kay, Margaret Kinstler, and others from Cabrillo College and our writing group.

The faculty, staff, and students in Seattle Pacific University's Master of Fine Arts program in Creative Writing modeled deep faith and commitment to great writing in all forms, especially my mentors Leslie Leyland Fields and Robert Clark, program director Gregory Wolfe, and my often roommate Carol Park.

Lisa Sadleir-Hart, Julie Scholz, and Teri Harbour O'Keefe connect me to childhood with the spirit's delicate threads. Georgann Turner, Denise Dupree, Tamera McCoskery, Joy Sprague, Nina Sprull, and the Amherst Writers and Artists group on Bainbridge Island root me to my new writing life in the Pacific Northwest.

Peggy Rosenthal, gifted writer for *Image* journal's "Good Letters" blog and poetry teacher, graciously reviewed this manuscript before I submitted it for publication. Chad Thomas Johnston, author of *Nightmarriage,* introduced me to eLectio publishing and has been a champion since we met through "Good Letters."

Not least, I am astounded by the deep blessings of my prayer partnership with Becky Perry and the wisdom of her gentle incisive spirit.

I invite you to visit my website: cathywarner.com to read more of my writing, and to hear several of these poems read aloud.

My life is overflowing with gifts. I pray that some of them will spill out in the world through these pages.

Made in the USA
San Bernardino, CA
13 January 2014